Step by Step Cuisine

Agnete Lampe

with Ulla Wetterholm

Translated by Ann Henning
Photography by Björn Lindberg

Ward Lock Limited · London

Text and Illustrations © 1977 Agnete Lampe/Femina, Helsingborg, Sweden

Translation © Ward Lock Limited 1978

First published in Great Britain in 1978
by Ward Lock Limited, 116 Baker Street,
London W1M 2BB, a member of the Pentos Group.

Translated by Ann Henning
Consultant cookery expert Audrey Ellison
House editor Eleanor-Mary Cadell

Phototypeset by Computer Photoset Limited, Birmingham
Printed in Great Britain by
Wm. Collins & Sons Limited, Glasgow and bound by
Richard Clay (The Chaucer Press) Limited, Bungay, Suffolk

British Library Cataloguing in Publication Data

Lampe, Agnete
    Step-by-step cuisine.
    1. Cookery
    I. Title   II. Wetterholm, Ulla
    641.5   TX717

    ISBN 0–7063–5420–6

Contents

Note

Metric and imperial measures are given for all the recipes in this book. These measures are not interchangeable. Either the metric or the imperial measure should be followed for successful results.

Bisque Ricardo

A delicious soup, easy to make with fresh, frozen or canned shellfish.

Serves 4–5

Dice onion, garlic and celery and fry in oil until soft but not brown.

2 Crush saffron in a mortar and fry for a little while. Add peeled and chopped tomatoes.

3 Add stock, wine, bay leaf, parsley, salt and pepper. Cover and simmer for 10 minutes.

4 Brush and scrape fresh mussels and rinse them under cold running water (throw away all those which do not close). Boil them separately in a little water until they open. Strain and reserve water.

5 Add prawns and mussels to the soup together with the strained water from the mussels. Add lemon and more seasoning to taste.

6 Remove from the heat. Whip the egg yolks with a little water and add to the mixture.

Minestrone Antoinetta

The Italians call minestrone the jewel of soups. If you make your own stock you have food for several days. The brisket can be served with horseradish sauce, and the leg of veal makes a good blanquette.

Serves 6–8

at you need:

tres/3½ pints	50 g/2 oz pasta
ood meat stock	1 teaspoon chervil
eks	1 teaspoon basil
carrots	Parmesan cheese,
nion	grated
arlic clove	
iece of turnip	**to make stock**
iece of white	1 kg/2 lb brisket of
abbage	beef
iece of celeriac	1 kg/2 lb leg of veal
ablespoon butter	3 litres/5 pints water
ablespoon oil	1½ tablespoons salt
ablespoons	15 white peppercorns
omato purée	1 bay leaf
easpoons	
aprika powder	

1 To make stock, place meat and bones in a large pan and cover with the cold water. Bring to the boil slowly and skim.

Add seasoning, the green of the leeks and one diced carrot. Simmer for 2–3 hours.

3 Strain the stock and skim off the fat.

4 Dice the remaining vegetables. Fry onion, garlic and leeks in butter and oil. Add tomato purée and paprika powder.

5 Allow to fry for a minute and then add stock.

6 Bring the soup to the boil and add the remaining vegetables.

7 Boil for 30 minutes. Add pasta and herbs and boil for another 15 minutes. Season to taste and serve with grated Parmesan cheese and perhaps some diced meat in the soup.

Balkan lamb soup

A rich and filling soup of lamb, onions, tomatoes, peppers and lentils.

Serves 4–5

What you need:

- almost 1 kg/2 lb shoulder and neck (or breast) of lamb
- onions
- garlic clove, crushed
- tablespoons butter or margarine
- tablespoon paprika powder
- tablespoon tomato purée
- can tomatoes
- litres/3 pints stock
- bay leaf
- teaspoon marjoram
- 250 g/8 oz lentils
- peppers
- salt and pepper

1 Cut the meat off the bones and dice. Prepare stock by boiling the bones.

2 Chop the onions and crush the garlic and fry in butter until soft but not brown. Remove from pan.

3 Brown the meat and sprinkle with the paprika. Return the onions to the pan with the tomato purée and the diced tomatoes.

4 Add the strained stock, bay leaf and marjoram. Cover the pan and simmer for 30 minutes.

5 Rinse the lentils in cold water, drain and add to the soup. Boil for another 20 minutes.

6 Add the sliced peppers, simmer for another 5 minutes and add seasoning to taste.

9

Scampi Indiana

Curried prawns with vegetables is an easy dish to make and always successful. The best results are achieved with fresh or frozen prawns.

Serves 4

hat you need:

 fresh or 400 g/1 lb frozen (preferably
raw) prawns
4 tablespoons oil
lt and pepper
ml/2 fl. oz brandy
blespoon curry powder
easpoon garlic powder
0 ml/8 fl. oz double cream
8 tomatoes
mall can pimientos
couple of drops of tabasco
ettuce

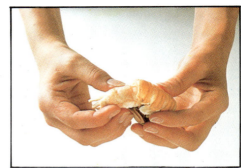

1 Peel the fresh prawns.

Heat the oil and fry the prawns
quickly. Season to taste.

3 Add brandy and light it with a
match.

4 Add curry and garlic powder and
stir in well while frying.

Add the cream.

6 Add tomato segments and sliced
pimiento, bring to the boil and
simmer slowly for 2–3 minutes.

7 Add seasoning, spices and tabasco
to taste. Serve with rice and garnish
with shredded lettuce.

11

Pâté de fruits de mer

In France a pâté is a meat or fish pie. This recipe is for one of the most delicious fish dishes you can imagine. The pie is easy to prepare in advance. It can be baked just before serving.

Serves 6

What you need:
_0 g/8 oz mushrooms
_0 g/1 lb prawn tails (scampi), frozen,
boiled or raw
_0–300 g/8–12 oz Dublin Bay prawns
_ablespoons butter
_easpoons curry powder
_0 ml/12 fl. oz dry white wine
_0 ml/8 fl. oz double cream
_ablespoons plain flour
_lt and pepper

_stry:
_0 g/1 lb plain flour
_0 g/8 oz butter
_easpoon salt
_tablespoons water
_tablespoons cream
_egg

Begin with the pastry. Rub the butter into the flour, add salt and then stir in water, blended with the cream and egg. Quickly mix the pastry and leave it in a cool place.

2 Slice mushrooms, dice the scampi and peel the prawns. Fry the mushrooms and unboiled scampi in half the butter, adding the curry powder.

3 Add wine and cream and boil for a couple of minutes. Mix the remaining butter with the flour, and add it to the mixture in pellets.

4 Add the prawns and boiled scampi, season to taste and leave the mixture to cool.

5 Roll out the pastry and line a greased oven-proof dish (28–30 cm/10–12 in in diameter) with half of it. Prick with a fork and add the shellfish mixture.

6 Brush the edge with egg, cover with the remaining pastry and trim. Press the edges together, brush with egg and decorate with pastry shapes. Make a couple of cuts in the lid and bake the pie at 200°C/400°F/gas mark 6 for 30 minutes. Serve with salad.

13

Moules d'Aunis

The fresh mussel is a delicacy worth some extra attention. This French recipe makes a delicious starter or snack.

Serves 2

at you need:
mussels
ml/8 fl. oz dry white wine
ml/4 fl. oz water
easpoon thyme
ay leaf
rsley

uce:
ablespoons chopped shallot or
onion
arlic clove, crushed
ablespoon olive or corn oil
ablespoon plain flour
easpoon curry powder
ml/8 fl. oz mussel stock
ml/2 fl. oz double cream
ch of cayenne pepper
easpoon lemon juice

Brush, scrape and rinse the mussels under running cold water and remove the tuft. Throw away all mussels that do not close.

2 Bring to the boil in a large pan the wine, water, thyme, bay leaf and parsley. Add the mussels.

3 Let the mussels boil vigorously under cover for 6–8 minutes until they open. Shake the pan in the meantime. Lift the mussels out of the pan. Strain and boil the stock.

To make the sauce, fry shallot or onion and garlic in oil, add flour, curry powder, mussel stock and cream. Add cayenne pepper and lemon to taste.

5 Remove one shell from each mussel and place them close together in an oven-proof dish.

6 Pour the sauce over them and serve immediately, or add some grated cheese and brown later.

1 Season the fish fillets and place them in a greased oven-proof dish.

Cut the onions into small segments, slice the mushrooms and the peppers. Fry them all together in oil for a few minutes.

3 Use a garlic press to add the garlic to the mixture.

4 Scald and skin the tomatoes, chop them and stir them in to the mixture.

Add lemon juice and some water. Season, add oregano and allow to simmer for a few minutes.

6 Pour the mixture over the fish.

7 Add a few knobs of butter and set the dish in the oven at 225°C/425°F/gas mark 7 for 15 minutes. Baste occasionally. Serve with boiled rice or potatoes.

23

Fredrik's baked fish

Haddock and cod are perfectly suitable for everyday meals. In this version, with herb butter and wine, they become festive fare. Frozen fillets are also acceptable; 800 g/2 lb frozen fillets can be substituted for 1½ kg/3 lb fresh fish on the bone.

Serves 4

What you need:

1.5 kg/3 lb haddock or cod
1 egg yolk
100 g/4 oz butter
2 tablespoons finely chopped onion
2 tablespoons finely chopped parsley
1 teaspoon dried tarragon
salt and pepper
1 thick slice of white bread
200–300 ml/8–12 fl. oz dry white wine

1 Scrape and rinse the fish. Slit from head to tail, cut up the belly and remove the entrails.

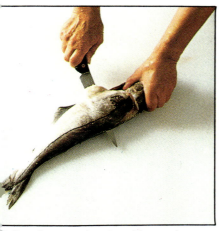

2 Cut from under the gill opening along the backbone down to the tail. With a sharp knife, separate the fish from the bone. Turn the fish and remove the other fillet.

3 Remove the dark membrane and small bones. Rinse the fillets.

4 Blend together egg yolk, butter, onions, parsley and tarragon until smooth.

5 Place the fish fillets in a greased oven-proof dish, add salt and pepper and spread the mixture over them.

6 Grate the bread over the fish in an even layer.

7 Pour in half of the wine at the side of the fish without moistening the surface. Put the dish near the top of the oven and bake for 15–20 minutes at 250°C/475°F/gas mark 9 adding more wine as necessary to prevent the fish drying out.

25

Truite farcie

Everybody will love this dish, because the trout is completely boneless, although it looks whole. The dish can be prepared beforehand and baked just before it is served.

Serves 4

What you need:

4 medium-sized trout
Salt and pepper
1 lemon
100 g/4 oz mushrooms
2 tomatoes
1 onion *or* 3–4 shallots
chives
parsley *or* dill
2 tablespoons soy sauce
2 tablespoons butter

1 Rinse and dry the trout and cut along either side of the backbone with a sharp knife.

2 Break off the bone at the head and draw the knife under the backbone, as closely as possible, towards the tail. Remove the backbone.

3 Remove all the small bones and rub the fish with salt, pepper and lemon.

4 Dice the mushrooms, tomatoes and onions. Fry together in butter and add chopped chives and chopped parsley.

5 Season and allow to cool. Divide the stuffing between the four trout.

6 Place the trout in a greased ovenproof dish and squeeze over a little lemon juice.

7 Brush the fish with a mixture of soy sauce and melted butter. Bake in the oven at 200°C/400°F/gas mark 6 for 15–20 minutes. Baste occasionally.

27

Anguilles au vert

'Anguilles au vert' is a well-known Flemish dish. Many Belgian fishmongers sell the herb mixture used for it. The eel must not be too large or thick.

Serves 4–5

...at you need:

...els, 500–600 g/1–1¼ lb each
...ablespoons butter
...–50 g/1¼–1¾ oz finely chopped herbs,
...such as parsley, chives, chervil and
...dill
...easpoon each dried thyme,
...arragon and sage
...t and pepper
...0 ml/6 fl. oz dry white wine
...ay leaf
...ablespoon plain flour
...gg yolks

Ask the fishmonger to skin and clean the eel and cut it into pieces 5 cm/2 in thick. Rinse, dry and remove the fins.

...lt the butter in a heavy pan. Add the ...and fry it but do not allow it to ...wn.

Add the dried herbs and half of the fresh ones.

Add salt, pepper, wine and bay leaf.

...ver and simmer for 15–20 minutes, ...n remove the eel and set aside.

Boil the stock and thicken with the flour, stirred to a thin cream with cold water.

Whisk in the egg yolks. Take the pan off the heat, remove the bay leaf and add the remaining herbs. Put the eel back in the pan and heat gently. Do not boil. Serve with potatoes or rice.

Paupiettes of plaice in aspic

Aspic is much easier to make than some of us think. This is a wonderful cool summer dish, served with herb mayonnaise.

Serves 6

hat you need:
0 g/2 lb plaice fillets (fresh or frozen)
0 g/1 lb prawns
ard-boiled egg
ll

aching liquid:
itre/2 pints water
ablespoon salt
ice of ½ lemon
white peppercorns
ay leaf
nion
ll

pic:
0 ml/1¾ pints fish stock
eaves of gelatine (or 2½ tablespoons
powdered gelatine)

Roll the fish fillets, skin inwards, and place them next to each other in a shallow pan.

2 Boil water, salt, lemon juice, peppercorns, bay leaf, sliced onion and dill for a few minutes and pour over the fish. Cover the pan and simmer for 10 minutes.

3 Put the gelatine leaves in water, squeeze, and melt over a low heat (or stir the gelatine powder with water to dissolve). Add fish stock. Pour a layer of aspic into a dish rinsed with water. Leave to set.

Garnish with sliced egg, prawns and dill when the aspic has set. 'Bind' with some aspic and leave to set.

5 Add the remaining prawns, cold fish and dill sprigs attractively arranged.

6 Add the remaining aspic and leave in a cool place until the aspic has set. Empty the dish on to a serving plate and serve with bread and mayonnaise or soured cream with lemon, seasoning and chives added to it.

Summer mackerel in wine

The silvery mackerel is one of the finest fishes available in summer. This is a practical and tasty dish made with cold mackerel and served with fresh summer vegetables and a delicious dill sauce.

Serves 5–6

What you need:

1.4 kg/3 lb whole fresh mackerel
1 lemon
1 carrot
1 onion
1 leek
4 sprigs or 1 teaspoon dried thyme
1 bay leaf
4 peppercorns
2 cloves
400–500 ml/16–20 fl. oz water
300 ml/16 fl. oz dry white wine
2 teaspoons salt

Garnish:

tomatoes
cucumber
lemon wedges
peas
dill

Remove the heads of the mackerel, slit along the belly of each fish and remove the entrails. Cut off the fins. Rinse and dry the fish.

2 Cut the mackerel into 3 cm/1½ in pieces.

3 Slice lemon, carrot, onion and leek. Mix with spices, water and wine, season and boil for 10 minutes.

4 Add the mackerel, cover and poach for 8 minutes. Let it cool in its own stock.

5 Lift out the fish, place it on a serving dish and pour a little of the stock over it.

6 Garnish with tomato sections, sliced cucumber, lemon wedges, peas and dill. Serve with boiled potatoes or bread and a sauce of half mayonnaise, half soured cream mixed with lemon juice, salt, pepper and finely chopped dill.

Truite en gêlée

Cold boiled trout in wine aspic, served with salad, sauce verte (see page 43), new potatoes and a glass of chilled white wine, is delicious on a hot summer's day.

Serves 4

hat you need:
medium-sized trout
0 ml/1½ pints fish stock (cube)
0 ml/12 fl. oz dry white wine
bay leaf
white peppercorns
allspice corns
ll sprigs

pic:
0 ml/1¼ pints fish stock
gelatine leaves (or 2 tablespoons
powdered gelatine)

arnish:
awns
ll
mon

Clean and rinse the fish. Boil the
fish stock with wine, dill,
seasoning and spices for about 10
minutes. Add the fish, cover the pan
and simmer for 10–12 minutes.

2 Lift out the fish, pull off the skins
and leave to cool in the stock.

3 Strain the stock. Soak the gelatine
leaves in cold water, squeeze and
melt them. (Stir the gelatine
powder with water to dissolve).
Mix the dissolved gelatine with the
fish stock.

Put the trout on a wire rack and
pour some of the semi-set aspic
over them.

5 Garnish with prawns, dill and
lemon.

6 Bind the garnish by covering with
the remaining aspic. Serve the trout
with salad, new potatoes and soured
cream mixed with dill and parsley.

Salmon pâté Wellington

I ate this delicious salmon pâté in the Wellington restaurant of the London Hilton hotel. Smoked salmon is expensive, but the pâté goes a long way, and tail trimmings of smoked salmon are sometimes sold at a lower price.

Serves 8–10

What you need:

350 g/12 oz smoked salmon (tail pieces)
100 g/4 oz fillet of smoked herring or buckling
350 g/12 oz cooked fillet of fish (plaice, sole or salmon)
50 ml/2 fl. oz water
juice of ½ lemon
2 tablespoons whisky
200 ml/8 fl. oz double cream
dill
50 g/2 oz butter

1 Remove all bones from the fish, cut it into pieces and put it through a mincer twice.

2 Add water, lemon juice and whisky and pound the mixture until smooth.

3 Whip the cream until stiff and fold it in to the minced fish.

4 Pour the mixture into a greased oven-proof dish and smooth the surface.

5 Cover with a lid or tin foil and bake standing in a water-bath in the oven at 175°C/325°F/gas mark 3 for 30–40 minutes.

6 Leave the pâté to cool a little. Garnish with dill and pour melted butter over it. Serve the pâté cold with toast and salad.

37

Lasagne con ricotta e spinati

Not only vegetarians will appreciate this lovely pasta dish, where the lasagne is filled with cottage cheese and spinach instead of the usual minced-meat mixture.

Serves 4

What you need:
12 sheets lasagne pasta
salt
2–3 tablespoons oil

Filling:
300–400 g/12–16 oz frozen chopped
  spinach
salt and pepper
grated nutmeg
100 g/4 oz ricotta or cottage cheese

Sauce:
2 garlic cloves
2 onions
2 × 450 g/1 lb can tomatoes
salt and pepper
1 teaspoon basil
10 black or green olives
4 tablespoons grated cheese

1 Boil the lasagne, a few at a time, in plenty of salted water with a little oil for 12 minutes. Lift them out and allow to drain.

2 Thaw the spinach, fry it lightly in oil, add salt, pepper and grated nutmeg and then add the ricotta or cottage cheese.

3 Fry the crushed garlic and chopped onion in oil. Add the chopped tomatoes, seasoning and spice and let the sauce boil uncovered for 10 minutes to reduce it.

4 Spread the spinach filling between the sheets of lasagne.

5 Roll them up and place the rolls, seam-side down, in a greased oven-proof dish.

6 Add sliced olives to the sauce and pour it over the pasta.

7 Sprinkle with grated cheese and bake in the oven at 200°C/400°F/ gas mark 6 for 20 minutes.

Sweetcorn and pepper soufflé

If you have never dared to attempt a soufflé before, begin with this one! It is slightly richer than ordinary soufflés, but delicious, and an ideal dish for a main course.

Serves 4

hat you need:

ablespoons butter or margarine
ablespoons plain flour
)ml/½ pint milk
ggs
5–175 g/5–7 oz grated cheese
an of sweetcorn with peppers
easpoon salt
ack pepper
ated nutmeg

Melt butter and flour together. Add milk and whisk the sauce until smooth.

2 Take the saucepan off the heat and whisk in the egg yolks.

3 Add the grated cheese, the well-drained sweetcorn and peppers. Add the spice and season to taste.

Whisk the egg whites until stiff and continue whisking for a further while.

5 Fold in half the whites, then the rest. Blend with care.

6 Pour the mixture into a soufflé dish lined with breadcrumbs. The dish should be deep and hold 1 litre/2 pints. Bake the soufflé at 170°C/ 325°F/gas mark 3 for 40 minutes. Serve with melted butter, tomato or mushroom sauce.

Artichokes with sauce verte

In France artichokes are often served with a variety of sauces, leaving each person a choice. The sauces can be lemon butter, French dressing, hollandaise sauce or herb mayonnaise (sauce verte), which is the one we have chosen for this recipe.

Serves 4

What you need:
4 artichokes
1 lemon

Sauce verte:
2 egg yolks
2 teaspoons vinegar
2 teaspoons mustard
1 teaspoon salt

Freshly ground black pepper
200 ml/8 fl. oz oil
100–200 ml/4–8 fl. oz soured cream
1 garlic clove
7 tablespoons finely chopped dill
Parsley
Chives

Hold the artichoke firmly by the stalk and break the stalk off so that the bottom leaves and the thick threads come away

Rub the bottom with lemon to prevent it from discolouring, put the artichokes in boiling salted water.

over and boil them for 30–40 minutes epending on their size. They are cooked hen the bottom leaves come off easily.

Take out the artichokes and put them upside down on a plate to drain.

While the artichokes are boiling, make the sauce. Whisk egg yolks, vinegar, mustard and seasoning for 2–3 minutes.

/hisk in the oil, drop by drop, until the auce is thick and smooth.

Then add the remaining oil in a steady stream. (If the mayonnaise curdles, put another egg yolk in a clean bowl and add the curdled mayonnaise a little at a time stirring continuously).

Add soured cream, crushed garlic and herbs and taste for seasoning.

What you need:

500 g/1¼ lb boiled ham
200 g/8 oz baked liver pâté
5 gelatine leaves (or 1½ tablespoons
    powdered gelatine)
200 ml/8 fl. oz double cream
500 ml/1 pint stock (cube) or
    consommé soup
Salt and pepper
Paprika
Celery salt
Mono sodium glutamate
Sherry or port

Garnish:
Red peppers
Small gherkins

1 Dice the ham, mince and mix with the liver pâté.

2 Put the gelatine leaves in cold water, squeeze them and melt over a low heat (or dissolve the powder in a little warm water). Add to the stock and then add 300 ml/12 fl. oz of the jellied stock and the cream to the meat.

3 Add seasoning, spices and sherry or port.

4 Pour 100 ml/4 fl. oz jellied stock into a plain ring mould rinsed with water, let it set and garnish with pepper and gherkins cut in half. Pour the rest of the stock over it and leave to set.

5 Add pats of the meat mixture with a spoon and smooth the surface. Leave the mould in a cold place until just before serving.

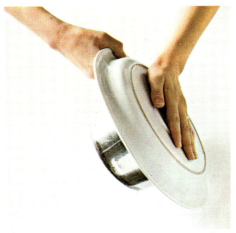

6 Dip the mould into hot water and turn out on to a serving dish. Serve the mousse with asparagus, peas, tomatoes, bread and butter.

Hare pâté Monsieur Henri

Hare pâté was originally a French dish. It is served cold as a snack or as a starter directly from the dish in which it was cooked. If you have the time to make it, it is an ideal party dish.

Serves 10–12

What you need:

[5]00 g/1 lb shoulder of pork
[1] skinned hare
[2]00 g/8 oz boiled ham
[1]00 g/4 oz fat bacon or pork fat (for
  larding)
[3] eggs
[4]–6 black olives
[s]alt and pepper
[1] teaspoon dried thyme
[1] bay leaf
[1]00 g/4 oz bacon

Marinade:

[1]00 ml/4 fl. oz brandy
[1] garlic clove, crushed
[2] teaspoons Epice Riche (2 parts
  mace, 2 parts white pepper, 1 part
  allspice, 1 part cloves)
[s]alt and pepper

1 Joint the hare, remove the meat from the bone and trim it. Finely slice the flesh from the saddle of the hare, the ham and the fat bacon and marinade for a few hours.

2 Mince all the meat and add eggs and chopped olives.

3 Add enough marinade to make a smooth mixture and season to taste.

4 Line an oven-proof dish with bacon rashers

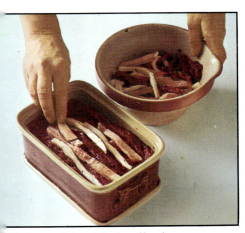

5 Cover this with the sliced meat and larding strips.

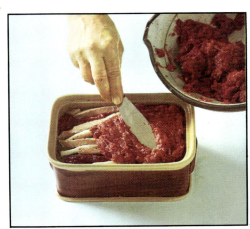

6 Arrange the layers of mince, sliced meat and larding strips so that the top layer is mince.

7 Cover with the remaining bacon rashers, crumble the thyme on top and insert the bay leaf. Cover the dish and bake the pâté in a water-bath in the oven at 200°C/400°F/gas mark 6 for about 1½ hours. Leave the pâté to cool and serve with redcurrant jelly.

71

Anna's terrine

Baked liver pâté can form a good, nourishing and inexpensive meal. Served in the Danish way with crisply fried bacon and mushrooms, it tastes delicious.

About 1 kg/2½ lb

What you need:

- 0g/1½ lb pig's liver
- 0g/1 lb fat bacon
- nion
- –12 anchovy fillets
- ablespoons butter or margarine
- ablespoons plain flour
- 0ml/16 fl. oz milk
- easpoon salt
- easpoon pepper
- easpoon ground allspice
- easpoon ground cloves
- ggs

Cut liver and larding bacon into pieces and mince twice with onion and anchovies in a mincer.

2 Fry the butter and flour to make a roux. Add boiling milk, whisk the sauce until smooth and add seasoning and spices.

3 Take the sauce off the heat and stir in eggs one at a time.

Add the liver mixture and blend well. Adjust seasoning to taste.

5 Pour the mixture into one large, or several small fire-proof dishes.

6 Cover with a lid or tin foil and bake in a water-bath in the oven at 200°C/400°F/gas mark 6 for about one hour. Remove the lid towards the end to brown the top.

Coq au vin

Anyone who has ever been to France must have tried this traditional dish, which is served everywhere.

Serves 4

What you need:

1 kg/2 lb chicken
2 tablespoons butter
1 tablespoon plain flour
350 ml/12 fl. oz stock
1 tablespoon tomato purée
50 g/2 oz belly of pork
100 g/4 oz baby onions
100 g/4 oz mushrooms
salt and pepper
parsley

Marinade:

1 bottle of red wine
1 carrot
1 onion
1 bay leaf
1 teaspoon thyme
1 sprig parsley

Joint the bird by first cutting off wings and legs. Cut the legs into two at the joint.

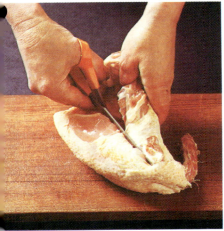

Cut the bird into two pieces—one breast and one back half.

Cut back and breast pieces into three.

Place the pieces in a bowl and pour the marinade over them. Marinade for a few hours or overnight.

Dry the pieces and brown in the butter in a pan. Add the onion and carrot from the marinade.

Add the flour, stock, tomato purée and 200 ml/8 fl. oz strained marinade.

Slice pork finely and brown. Brown shallots and mushrooms and add to the pan. Cover and simmer for 30–40 minutes. Season to taste and garnish with chopped parsley. Serve with boiled rice.

75

Tandoori chicken

This Indian speciality is one of the most delicious dishes I have ever tasted. The chicken is marinated in a spicy sauce and grilled until brown and crisp.

Serves 2

What you need:
1 fresh chicken, about 800 g/2 lb
2-3 garlic cloves
1 teaspoon ground ginger
1 teaspoon paprika
1 teaspoon ground coriander
2 teaspoons turmeric
1 teaspoon ground cumin seeds
2 teaspoons salt
juice of ½ lemon
200 ml/8 fl. oz yoghurt or single cream

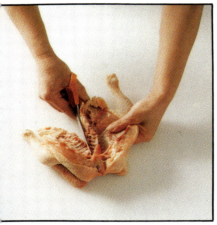

Cut the chicken into two halves by first cutting along the breast bone.

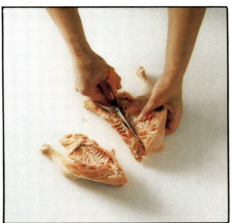

2 Cut away the backbone.

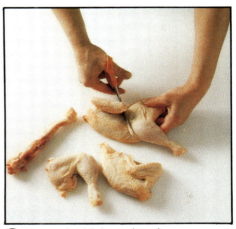

3 Cut each chicken piece into two— one breast and one leg.

4 Crush the garlic cloves and add to the yoghurt together with the spices and lemon juice.

5 Turn the chicken pieces in this mixture and leave in a cold place for 4 hours or more, turning them occasionally.

6 Grill the chicken over glowing charcoal or a radiation grill for about 20 minutes. First grill the skin sides, then turn the pieces. Finally, grill the skin sides again just before serving to make them crisp.

Almond apple pie

An ideal dessert. It should be served warm with vanilla ice cream or lightly whipped cream.

Serves 8–10

at you need:
g/5¼ oz plain flour
g/4 oz butter
blespoons sugar
blespoons cold water

ng:
g/4 oz almond paste
g/4 oz butter
firm sour apples
/2 oz caster sugar
rge egg whites

1 Rub the butter into the flour and sugar. Stir in the water and mix to a stiff dough. Leave the pastry in a cold place for a while and then line an oven-proof dish (about 24 cm/10 in diameter) with the pastry.

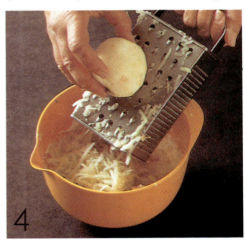

2 m the excess pastry along the edge and ck the pastry with a fork.

3 Grate the almond paste over the pastry case. Cream butter and sugar together until the mixture is fluffy.

4 Grate the apples and mix them with the creamed butter and sugar.

5 refully add the egg whites, whisked fly.

6 Spread the mixture over the almond paste.

7 Cover with strips of pastry, brush with a little beaten egg and bake the pie at 220°C/425°F/gas mark 7 for 35–40 minutes.

Suzy's lemon meringue pie

A deliciously refreshing dessert from America.

Serves 6

What you need:
175g/6oz butter
150g/5¼oz plain flour
3–4 tablespoons cold water

Filling:
4 egg yolks
2 tablespoons cornflour
150ml/6fl. oz water
100g/4oz caster sugar
Grated rind of 2 lemons
2–3 tablespoons lemon juice
2 teaspoons butter

Meringue:
4 egg whites
Just over 50g/2oz caster sugar
2 teaspoons lemon juice

1 Blend butter and flour, add water and work together lightly to bind the pastry dough and leave in a cold place.

2 Line a greased pie dish (22cm/9in in diameter) with the rolled out pastry. Prick the pastry case with a fork and place a strip of tin foil around the inside edge. Bake the pie at 240°C/475°F/gas mark 9 for 10 minutes. Remove the foil strip.

3 Whisk the cornflour, water and sugar together and let the mixture simmer until it thickens. Place the saucepan in hot water and stir in the egg yolks.

4 Add lemon rind, juice and butter, whisk the mixture until smooth. Leave to cool.

5 Spread the mixture over the baked pastry.

6 Whisk the egg whites until stiff. Add the sugar and continue whisking for a few minutes. Add a few drops of lemon juice.

7 Pile the meringue over the pie and bake at 170°C/325°F/gas mark 3 for 8–10 minutes. Serve the pie cold.

Bombe Alaska

This sweet dish is easier to cook than one would think, since it consists of a ready-made sponge-cake base, topped with ice cream, tinned fruit and meringue. All you have to make yourself is the meringue, which is, after all, quite an art in itself.

Serves 6

1 Place the sponge cake base on an oven-proof plate or a silver platter and soak it in liqueur and a little fruit syrup.

2 Cover with fruit and leave the plate in a cold place.

3 Whisk the egg whites until stiff, add the sugar and continue whisking for another ten minutes. (You can prepare the dish to this stage in advance).

Just before serving, scoop out the ice cream, which should be frozen hard, and place on top of the fruit.

5 Spread the meringue mixture over it. Make absolutely sure it covers all the ice cream and that no gaps are left.

6 Decorate with flaked almonds. Bake in the oven at 240°C/475°F/gas mark 9 until the meringue is slightly browned. Serve immediately.

83

Maraschino ice gâteau

This is the most glamorous and tasty finale to a special meal that one can imagine. This ice cream gâteau can be prepared in advance and then frozen.

Serves 10

What you need:

egg whites
g/2¾ oz caster sugar
g/1 oz icing sugar
0 g/4 oz milled nuts
family-sized block strawberry ice
cream
ml/2½ fl. oz maraschino or kirsch
0 g/4 oz maraschino cherries
0 g/4 oz candied fruit
0 ml/12 fl. oz double cream

Whisk the egg whites stiffly, add the caster sugar a little at a time and finally the icing sugar.

2 Add the milled nuts and blend well.

3 Pipe the mixture on greaseproof paper to form two round bases and bake these at 100–130°C/180–250°F/ gas mark ¼–1 for 30–40 minutes.

4 Mix the ice cream and maraschino or kirsch and add the chopped fruit leaving some aside for decorating.

5 Place one base on a serving plate and cover with ice cream.

6 Place the other meringue case on top and spread half the whipped cream over it.

7 Pipe the remaining cream on top.

8 Decorate with remaining maraschino cherries and candied fruit.

9 Place the gâteau in your deep freeze for a few minutes before serving.

Danish strawberry cornets

Children adore them and adults too: crisp cones with cream and strawberries. A lovely sweet course!

20 cones

What you need:

100 g/4 oz butter or margarine
100 g/4 oz icing sugar
2 egg whites
100 g/4 oz plain flour

Filling:
Double cream (whipping cream)
Fresh or frozen strawberries or jam

1 Blend butter and sugar together until light and fluffy. Fold in the stiffly beaten egg whites.

2 Sift in the flour and mix carefully.

3 Spread the mixture as thinly and evenly as possible on greased and floured baking sheets in circles, 12 cm/4½ in in diameter. Mark rings around the circles of dough.

4 Bake the circles at 220°C/425°F/gas mark 7 for 4–5 minutes. Loosen them immediately with a sharp knife and shape them into cones. If the circles have become too cool to shape, put the baking sheet back into the oven for a moment.

5 Place the cones in narrow little glasses to keep their shape until they cool.
Place the cones in a bowl (they stand more firmly if there is some sugar at the bottom of the bowl).

6 Fill them with whipped cream mixed with mashed strawberries or jam just before serving and decorate with strawberry halves. The cones should be stored in an airtight tin in a dry place so that they remain crisp if they are not to be used at once.

Croissants

Morning coffee in France – or at home – is made perfect with fresh, warm, flaky croissants. They are also delicious served with consommé.

24 croissants

What you need:
5 g/½ oz yeast
50 ml/2 fl. oz water
425 g/1 lb plain flour
300 ml/12 fl. oz milk
2 teaspoons salt
2 tablespoons sugar
175 g/7 oz butter
1 egg

1 Dissolve the yeast in tepid water. Stir in 60 g/2½ oz of the flour and leave the dough to rise to double its size.

2 Make a dough of the remaining flour (save some for rolling out the dough), milk, salt and sugar and blend the two doughs together.

3 Roll out the dough on a floured board into a square about 1 cm/½ in thick.

4 Place thin slices of cold butter over one half of the dough.

5 Fold over the other half, press the edge lightly and roll it out to form a long piece of dough. Fold the dough three times and leave it in a cold place for 20 minutes. Fold and roll the dough twice further and leave it in a cold place between the foldings and rollings.

6 Leave the dough in a cold place for 4 hours or overnight. Roll it out until ½ cm/¼ in thick and cut it into 10 cm/4 in wide strips.
Cut the strips into pieces 10 cm/4 in long and divide them crosswise to form triangles. Roll up the triangles –pull the top corner slightly– and shape them into croissants.

7 Leave the croissants to swell to three times their volume. Brush with beaten egg and bake at 240°C/ 475°F/gas mark 9 for 12 minutes.

Plaited sesame bread

A nice loaf which looks and tastes as bread should.

What you need:
25 g/1 oz yeast
250 ml/½ pint skimmed milk or water
1 egg
2 tablespoons olive oil
1 teaspoon salt
1 tablespoon sugar
350–400 g/12–14 oz plain flour

To glaze:
1 egg
Sesame seeds

1 Crumble the yeast and dissolve it in a little of the tepid water. Add egg, oil, salt, sugar and the remaining water.

2 Add the flour, a little at a time, and work the dough until it comes away from the sides of the bowl. Leave to rise for 30 minutes.

3 Knead the dough on a floured board. Cut off one third. Then cut each piece into three and roll the pieces into 30 cm/12 in long rolls.

4 Put the largest rolls next to each other and plait them starting at the middle.

5 Place the finished plait on greaseproof paper on a baking sheet and flatten slightly.

6 Plait the smaller rolls in the same way and place them on top of the large plait. Flatten the plaits slightly. Leave to rise for 20 minutes.

7 Brush with beaten egg and sprinkle with sesame seeds. Bake at 200°C/400°F/gas mark 6 for 35–40 minutes.

Karin's cumin-seed bread

Light rye bread flavoured with cumin seeds is delicious served with salads or soups.

hat you need:
0 g/1 lb rye flour
0 g/10 oz plain flour
lt
ablespoon cumin seeds
g/2 oz yeast
0 ml/½ pint water
0 ml/½ pint cultured buttermilk

1 Mix the rye flour and plain flour with the salt and cumin seeds.

2 Crumble the yeast, pour tepid water over it and stir until the yeast dissolves. Add the buttermilk and blend with half the flour mixture.

3 Add the remaining flour a little at a time, but set aside 7 tablespoons for rolling the dough out.

4 Cover the dough with a greased plastic bag and let it rise until doubled in size. Knead the dough on a floured surface and divide into four pieces.

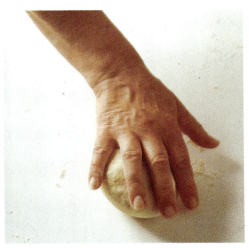

5 Knead each piece to form a smooth ball.

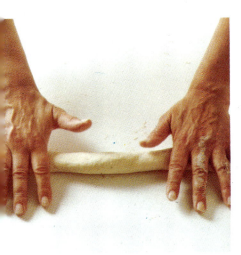

6 Roll out each ball into a long strip and place on greaseproof paper on a baking sheet.

7 Snip the dough on both sides and leave it to rise for about 30 minutes.

8 Brush the loaves with water, sprinkle with cumin seeds and bake at 220°C/ 425°F/gas mark 6 for 15 minutes.

Agnete's brown bread

A home-made brown loaf is always a pleasure to eat. It is good for everyday meals or for the most special occasions.

What you need :
g/2 oz yeast
ml/1½ pints milk
–400 g/12–14 oz plain flour
g/12 oz rye meal
aspoons salt

1 Crumble the yeast in a bowl. Heat the milk until it is tepid and pour over the yeast. Stir until the yeast has dissolved.

Sift the flour and the rye meal and salt and add most of it to the bowl.

3 Knead the dough and gradually add the rest of the flour mixture. Cover with a greased plastic bag and leave to rise until doubled in size for 40–60 minutes.

4 Place the dough on a floured board, knead until smooth and shape into a long loaf.

Place the loaf on greaseproof paper on a baking sheet and cut strips on the top with a razor blade.

6 Sift some flour over it.

7 Cover with a towel and let it rise for 20–30 minutes. Bake at 200°C/400°F/gas mark 6 for about 50 minutes. Let the loaf cool under a cloth if you like the crust soft and without the cloth if you prefer it crisp.

95